Mifflin
Harcourt

Science

Grade 1

Printed in the U.S.A.

ISBN   978-0-544-26186-0

8 9 10   0982   22 21 20 19 18 17

4500641105   B C D E F G

Science

Grade 1

Core Skills Science
GRADE 1
Table of Contents

Introduction

The *Core Skills Science* series offers parents and educators high-quality, curriculum-based products that align with the Next Generation Science Standards* Disciplinary Core Ideas for grades 1–8. The *Core Skills Science* series provides informative and grade-appropriate readings on a wide variety of topics in life, earth, and physical science. Two pages of worksheets follow each reading passage. The book includes:

• clear illustrations, making scientific concepts accessible to young learners

• engaging reading passages, covering a wide variety of topics in life, earth, and physical science

• logically sequenced activities, transitioning smoothly from basic comprehension to higher-order thinking skills

• comprehension questions, ascertaining that students understand what they have read

• vocabulary activities, challenging students to show their understanding of scientific terms

• critical thinking activities, increasing students' ability to analyze, synthesize, and evaluate scientific information

• questions in standardized-test format, helping prepare students for state exams

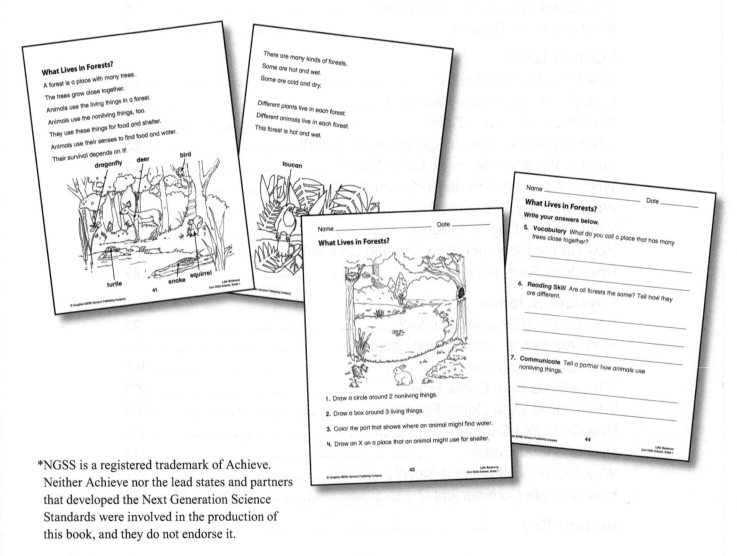

*NGSS is a registered trademark of Achieve. Neither Achieve nor the lead states and partners that developed the Next Generation Science Standards were involved in the production of this book, and they do not endorse it.

What Are the Parts of Plants?

Plants have parts.

Each part helps in a different way.

Roots take in water.

Roots hold the plant in the ground.

A stem joins parts of plants.

Stems carry water from the roots to other parts.

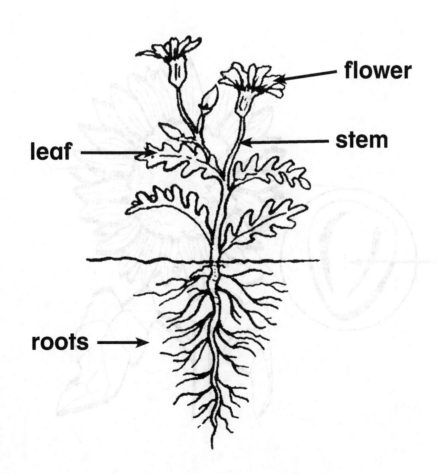

1

Most plants have leaves.

Leaves make food for the plant.

Leaves also make oxygen.

Plants and animals need oxygen.

Many plants have flowers.

A flower makes seeds.

New plants grow from seeds.

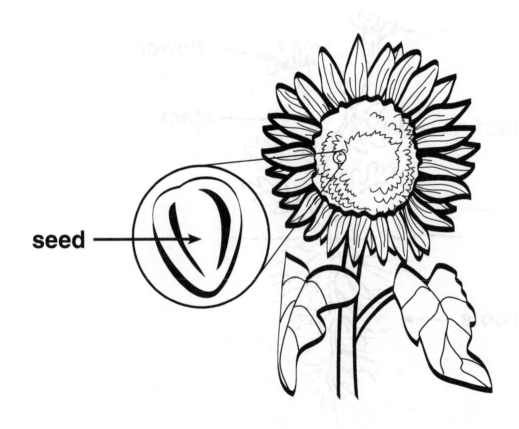

seed

Name _____ Date _____

What Are the Parts of Plants?

Draw a line from each definition to a part of the plant.

1. Takes in water from the ground

2. Connects roots to other plant parts

3. Makes food

4. Makes seeds

Underline the word that makes the sentence true.

5. (Stems, Leaves) carry water from the roots to other plant parts.

6. (Flowers, Leaves) give off oxygen that people and animals breathe.

Life Science
Core Skills Science, Grade 1

Name _____ Date _____

What Are the Parts of Plants?

Write your answers below.

7. **Vocabulary** What are **roots**?

    Roots take in water and hold the
    plant in the ground.

8. **Reading Skill** Why are a plant's roots under the ground?

    The roots take in water and
    hold the plant in the ground.

9. **Observe** Which plant parts can you observe above the ground?

    The parts I can observe are
    the leaves, stem and flower.

Life Science
Core Skills Science, Grade 1

How Can Plants Be Sorted?

You can sort plants.

You can put plants in groups by their parts.

Some plants have sharp points called spines.

A cactus has spines.

Some plants have flat leaves.

Many indoor plants have flat leaves.

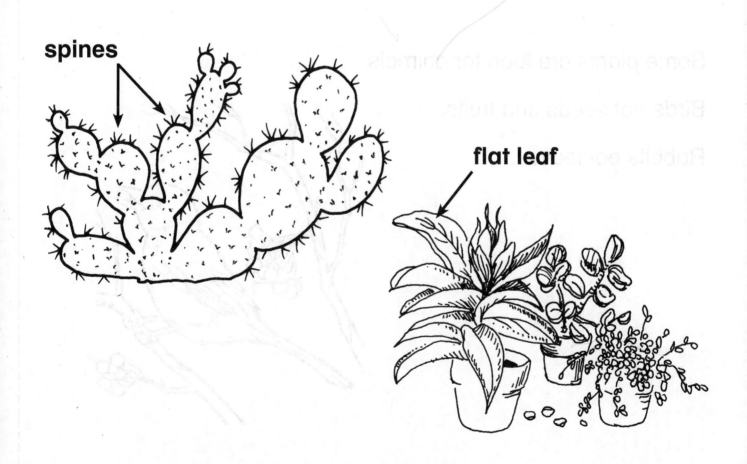

spines

flat leaf

Life Science
Core Skills Science, Grade 1

Some plants are food for people.

People eat leaves.

Lettuce is a leaf.

People eat fruit.

An apple is a fruit.

Some plants are food for animals.

Birds eat seeds and fruits.

Rabbits eat leaves.

Life Science
Core Skills Science, Grade 1

How Can Plants Be Sorted?

Draw a line from each sentence to its picture.

1. This plant has spines.

2. This plant has flat leaves.

Underline the word that makes the sentence true.

3. You can sort plants by looking at their (pots, parts).

4. Some plants are food for (other plants, people).

5. Some animals eat (seeds, spines) for food.

How Can Plants Be Sorted?

Write your answers below.

6. **Vocabulary** What kind of plant has **spines**?

_____

7. **Reading Skill** What are three plant parts that animals eat?

_____

_____

8. **Compare** How are plants different?

_____

_____

_____

How Do Plants Change as They Grow?

Pine trees start as seeds.

Pine seeds are in a cone.

A seed grows into a seedling.

The seedling grows into a tree.

The tree grows cones.

Seeds are in the cones.

Pine trees start as seeds.

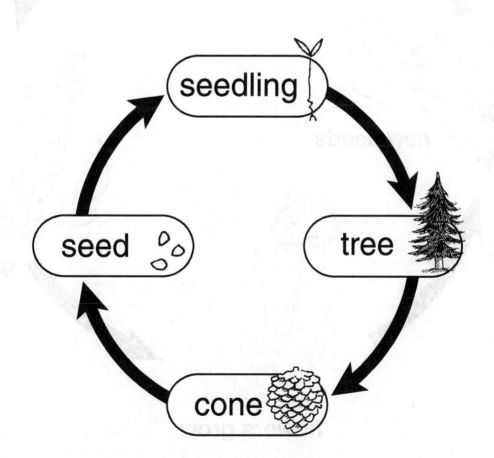

Changes in plants and animals happen in an order called a
life cycle.

Different plants have different life cycles.

Look at the picture.

The picture shows the life cycle of a plant.

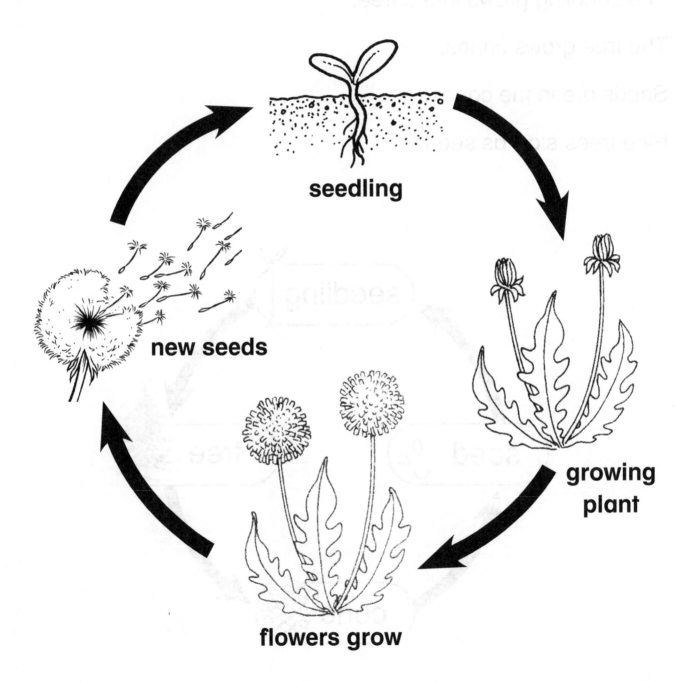

seedling

new seeds

growing
plant

flowers grow

10

How Do Plants Change as They Grow?

1. Draw a box around the picture of a cone.

2. Circle the picture of a seedling.

3. Draw a triangle around some seeds.

Name _____ Date _____

How Do Plants Change as They Grow?

Write your answers below.

4. **Vocabulary** What is a cone?

_____

_____

5. **Reading Skill** What comes after the seed in a plant's life cycle?

_____

_____

6. **Observe** How can a picture help you learn about a plant's life cycle?

_____

_____

_____

How Do Plants Change During Their Life Cycles?

All living things grow, change, and die.

The changes that a living thing goes through are its life cycle.

Not all plants have the same life cycle.

Flowering plants start from a seed planted in soil.

A seed grows into a young plant called a seedling.

Then the plant grows flowers that make fruits with seeds inside.

Later the fruit and seeds fall to the ground.

New plants can grow from these seeds.

The cycle of growing and changing will start again.

Plants are much like their parent plants.

They have the same kinds of leaves and seeds and fruits.

But different plants of the same kind can vary in the way they look.

Acorns are the fruit of an oak tree.

Acorns fall to the ground.

The seeds inside may grow new plants.

The seedlings may not be the same size and shape.

But the seedlings grow into the same kind of tree.

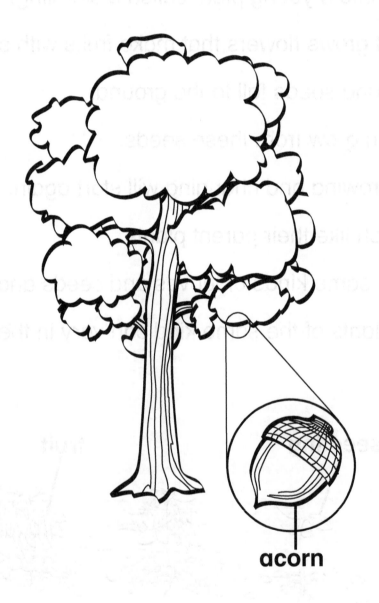

acorn

How Do Plants Change During Their Life Cycles?

Write numbers 1–5 on the line to show the life cycle of a bean plant.

_____ The young plant sprouts.

_____ The plant makes flowers.

_____ A seed is planted in the soil.

_____ The seeds fall to the ground.

_____ Flowers make seeds.

6. Draw a box around the picture of the seedling.

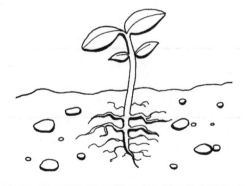

Name _____ Date _____

Write your answers below.

7. **Vocabulary** What is a life cycle?

_____

_____

_____

8. **Reading Skill** What happens to the seeds that are formed from a flower?

_____

_____

_____

9. **Compare** How is a seedling different from a grown plant?

_____

_____

_____

Life Science
Core Skills Science, Grade 1

How Do Animals Use Their Parts?

Animals have body parts.

Some body parts help
animals find food.

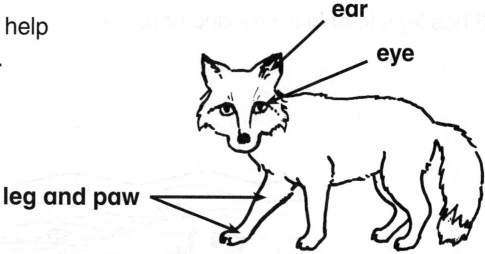

ear

eye

leg and paw

Some body parts help
animals stay safe.

stinger

Some body parts help
animals hide.

fur color

17

Some body parts help animals move.

A bird has wings to help it fly.

It has legs to help it walk and hop.

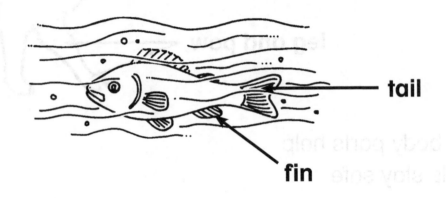

A fish has a tail and fins to help it swim.

A lion has legs to help it run fast.

How Do Animals Use Their Parts?

_____ _____ _____

_____ _____ _____

1. Write the word *wings* under the animal that has wings.

2. Write the word *fins* under the animal that has fins.

3. Write the word *legs* under the animals that have legs.

4. Write the word *swim* under the animal that lives in water.

5. Write the word *run* under the animal that can run.

How Do Animals Use Their Parts?

Write your answers below.

6. **Vocabulary** How do fins help a fish?

_____

_____

7. **Reading Skill** What body parts help
   an animal find food?

_____

_____

8. **Infer** How does a stinger help an animal stay safe?

_____

_____

Which Baby Animals Look Like Their Parents?

All living things grow and change.

All living things reproduce, too.

When living things reproduce, they make more living things of the same kind.

Offspring are the living things that come from the same living thing.

Animals are very much like their parents.

Animals of the same kind may vary a little. Children are the offspring of their parents.

Kittens are the offspring of their parents.

Offspring have the same body parts as their parents when they are born.

But they are different in some ways.

The hair or fur of the offspring may be a different color than the hair or fur of the parents.

21

Different kinds of animals have different life cycles.

Mice have young that look like their parents.

A mother mouse gives birth to live baby mice.

Soon the baby mice grow more fur.

The young mice grow up and can reproduce.

Birds have young that look like their parents, too.

A mother bird lays eggs.

The baby birds grow inside the eggs.

Chicks hatch from the eggs.

Soon the chicks get new feathers.

The young birds grow up and can reproduce.

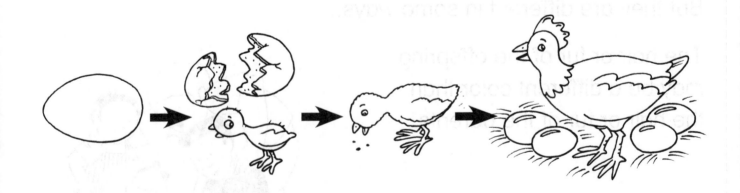

Life Science
Core Skills Science, Grade 1

Name _____ Date _____

Which Baby Animals Look Like Their Parents?

Match the sentences to the picture of the bird life cycle.
Write the letters on the lines.

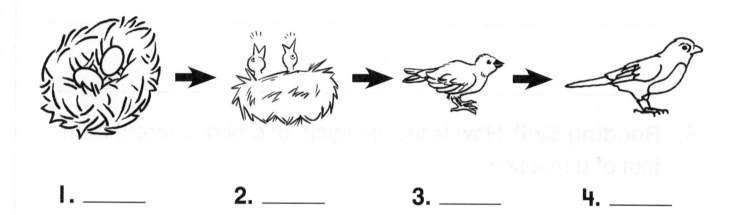

1. _____   2. _____   3. _____   4. _____

A. The chick gets new feathers as it grows.

B. A chick hatches from an egg. A parent feeds it.

C. The young bird grows up. It can reproduce.

D. A mother bird lays eggs. A chick grows inside.

Name _____ Date _____

Write your answers below.

5. **Vocabulary** What do living things do when they make more living things of the same kind?

_____

_____

6. **Reading Skill** How is the life cycle of a bird different from that of a mouse?

_____

_____

_____

7. **Compare** How are cat offspring alike and different from their parents?

_____

_____

_____

Which Baby Animals Do Not Look Like Their Parents?

Some baby animals do not look like their parents.

Young amphibians, like frogs, look different from their parents.

When they grow up, they will look like their parents.

A frog lays eggs in water.

When the eggs hatch, tadpoles come out.

They have gills and a tail that help them live in water.

Soon the tadpoles will grow back legs and lungs.

They need these parts to live on land.

The gills and tail will disappear.

The frogs will grow to look like their parents.

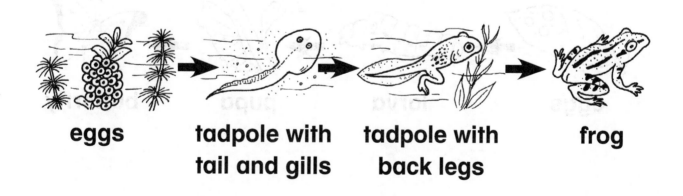

eggs   **tadpole with tail and gills**   **tadpole with back legs**   **frog**

Life Science
Core Skills Science, Grade 1

Butterflies belong to an animal group called insects.

Most insects change form as they grow.

A butterfly lays eggs on a plant.

A larva comes out of the egg.

A larva looks like a worm.

The larva eats leaves and grows and grows.

Then it changes form and turns into a pupa.

The pupa makes a special place where it can grow wings and legs.

The pupa does not eat or move.

When the change is done, a butterfly comes out.

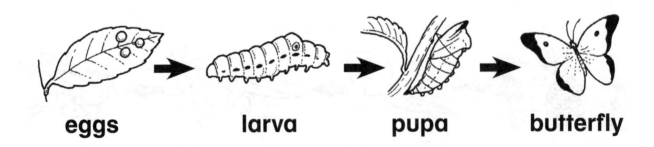

eggs   **larva**   **pupa**   **butterfly**

Name _____ Date _____

Which Baby Animals Do Not Look Like Their Parents?

Draw a line from each word to its picture.

1. egg

A.

2. tadpole

B.

3. adult

C.

4. larva

D.

5. pupa

E.

Name _____ Date _____

Write your answers below.

6. **Vocabulary** What is a larva?

_____

_____

_____

7. **Reading Skill** How are the life cycles of a frog and a butterfly different?

_____

_____

_____

8. **Infer** What happens to a frog after it grows parts for living on land?

_____

_____

_____

What Can People Do?

People have many body parts.

Body parts help you do things.

You use your arms to hug.

You use your legs to walk.

Some body parts help you learn what is around you.

These body parts are your senses.

You have five senses.

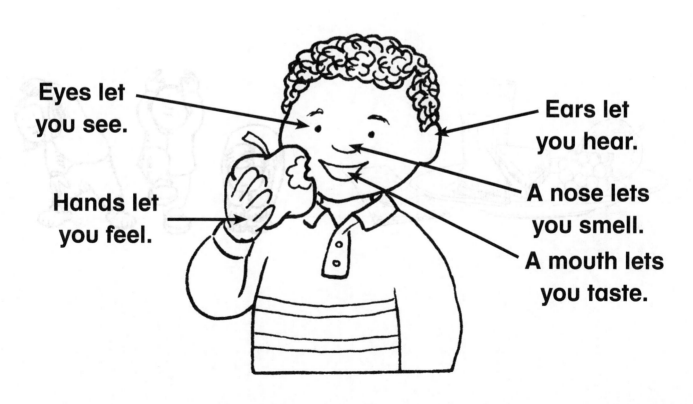

Eyes let you see.

Ears let you hear.

Hands let you feel.

A nose lets you smell.

A mouth lets you taste.

People grow and change.

First you were a baby.

Then you grew to be a child.

Someday you will become an adult.

You must stay healthy to keep growing.

You need to eat good food.

You need to exercise to be strong.

You need to sleep to rest your body and mind.

Name _____ Date _____

What Can People Do?

Draw a line to show the body part being used.

1.     **see**

2.     **hear**

3.     **taste**

4.    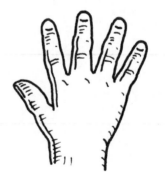 **feel**

5.     **smell**

Life Science
Core Skills Science, Grade 1

Name _____ Date _____

What Can People Do?

Write your answers below.

6. **Vocabulary** What is one kind of exercise?

_____

_____

7. **Reading Skill** How can you stay healthy?

_____

_____

8. **Work Together** Talk to a friend about how a baby is different from an adult.

_____

_____

_____

What Is a Living Thing?

A living thing grows and changes.

It makes other living things that are like it.

It needs air and food.

It needs water and space.

People and animals are living things.

Trees and grass are living things, too.

Some things are not alive.

They are nonliving things.

A nonliving thing does not eat or drink.

It does not grow.

It does not make other living things that are like it.

It does not need air, food, and water.

nonliving thing   **living thing**

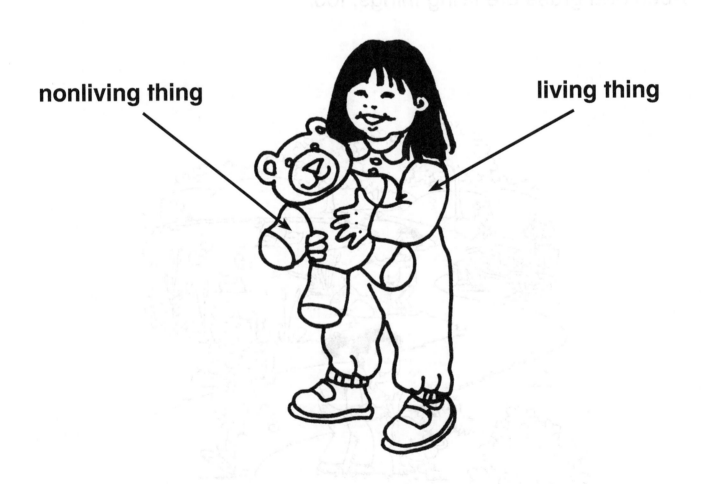

Life Science
Core Skills Science, Grade 1

What Is a Living Thing?

Draw a line from each sentence to its picture.

1. Living things grow and
change.

2. Living things need food.

3. Living things need water.

4. Living things make other
living things.

Life Science
Core Skills Science, Grade 1

What Is a Living Thing?

Write your answers below.

5. **Vocabulary** What is a living thing?

_____

_____

6. **Reading Skill** Name three nonliving things.

_____

_____

7. **Classify** Is water a living thing or a nonliving thing? Explain your answer.

_____

_____

_____

36

Life Science
Core Skills Science, Grade 1

What Do Living Things Need?

Plants and animals need food.

Plants use sunlight, air, and water to make their own food.

Some animals eat plants.

Some animals eat other animals.

Many animals eat both plants and animals.

Plants and animals
need water.

Most plants get water
from the ground.

Many animals get
water by drinking.

Plants and animals need air.

Animals breathe air.

Plants use air to make food.

Plants and animals need space.

Plants need space to grow.

Animals need space to find food.

Animals need shelter.

Shelter is a safe place to live.

Name _____ Date _____

What Do Living Things Need?

1. Circle the picture that shows what plants need to make food.

2. Draw a plus sign (+) on the picture that shows an animal getting food.

3. Draw a line through the picture that shows an animal finding shelter.

4. Draw a box around the picture that shows an animal getting water.

Life Science
Core Skills Science, Grade 1

Name _____ Date _____

What Do Living Things Need?

Write your answers below.

5. **Vocabulary** What kinds of **food** do animals eat?

_____

_____

6. **Reading Skill** What do plants need to live?

_____

_____

7. **Observe** Look at the picture.
What need is the child taking
care of?

_____

_____

What Lives in Forests?

A forest is a place with many trees.

The trees grow close together.

Animals use the living things in a forest.

Animals use the nonliving things, too.

They use these things for food and shelter.

Animals use their senses to find food and water.

Their survival depends on it!

dragonfly   **deer**   **bird**

turtle   **snake**   **squirrel**

Life Science
Core Skills Science, Grade 1

There are many kinds of forests.

Some are hot and wet.

Some are cold and dry.

Different plants live in each forest.

Different animals live in each forest.

This forest is hot and wet.

toucan

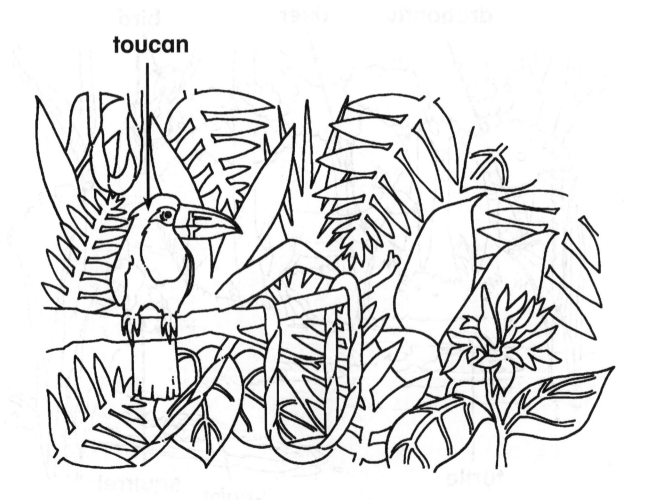

What Lives in Forests?

1. Draw a circle around 2 nonliving things.

2. Draw a box around 3 living things.

3. Color the part that shows where an animal might find water.

4. Draw an X on a place that an animal might use for shelter.

Name _____ Date _____

What Lives in Forests?

Write your answers below.

5. **Vocabulary** What do you call a place that has many trees close together?

_____

_____

6. **Reading Skill** Are all forests the same? Tell how they are different.

_____

_____

_____

7. **Communicate** Tell a partner how animals use nonliving things.

_____

What Lives in Oceans and Wetlands?

An ocean is a large body of salty water.

Animals and plants live in the ocean.

Ocean animals have special parts to

help them live in water.

Fish have fins and tails to swim.

They have gills to breathe.

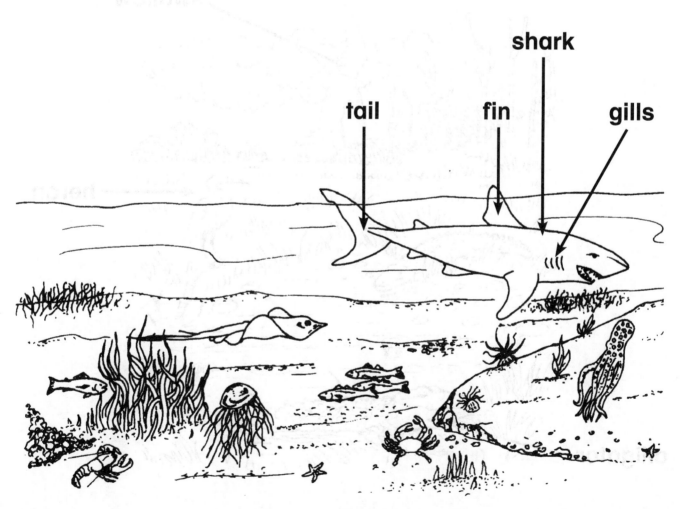

shark

tail   fin   gills

45

A wetland is land that is very wet.

There is mud in a wetland.

Many kinds of plants and animals live in a wetland.

The animals use their senses to find food and water in the mud, water, and plants.

Their survival depends on these things.

They find shelter in the mud, water, and plants.

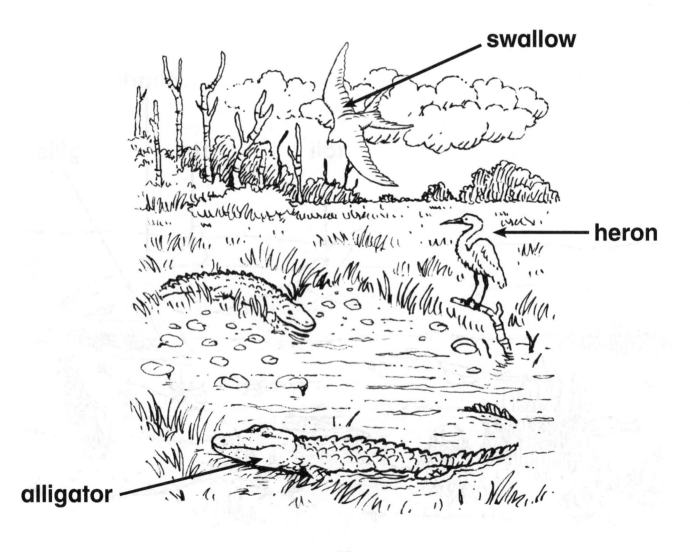

swallow

heron

alligator

46

Name _____ Date _____

What Lives in Oceans and Wetlands?

1. Draw a box around the ocean animals.

2. Draw a circle around the wetland animals.

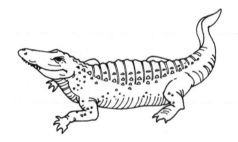 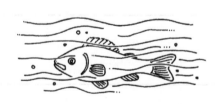 

Life Science
Core Skills Science, Grade 1

Name _____ Date _____

What Lives in Oceans and Wetlands?

Write your answers below.

3. **Vocabulary** What is a large body of salty water called?

_____

4. **Reading Skill** How are oceans different from wetlands?

_____

_____

_____

5. **Compare** How are oceans like wetlands?

_____

_____

What Lives in a Desert?

A desert is a hot place with very little water.

It can be hard to find food and water.

It is hot during the day.

It is cool at night.

Many animals sleep during the day.

They look for food at night.

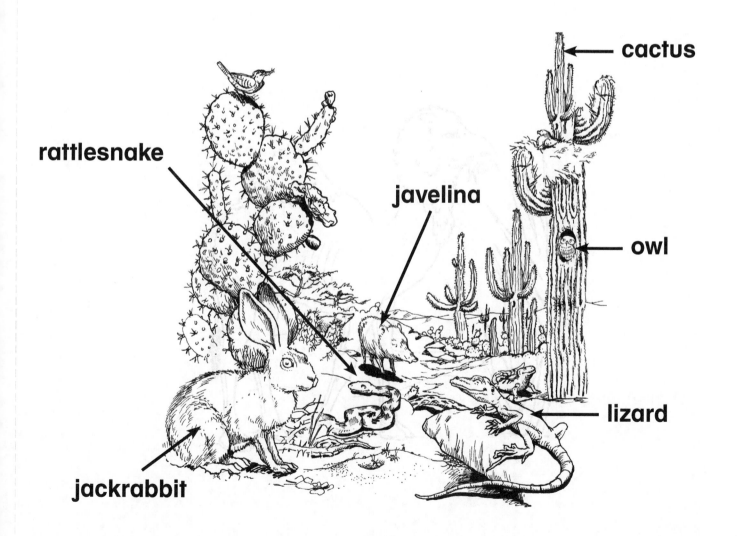

cactus

rattlesnake

javelina

owl

lizard

jackrabbit

Life Science
Core Skills Science, Grade 1

Desert plants and animals have special parts.

The parts help them live in dry places.

A cactus has thick stems.

It has waxy skin.

The stems and skin hold water.

A camel has wide feet.

Its feet help it walk in the sand.

50

Name _____ Date _____

What Lives in a Desert?

Label each picture with a word from the box.

cactus	owl	rattlesnake	jackrabbit

1.

2.

3.

4.

_____ _____ _____ _____

Underline the word that makes the sentence true.

5. A (desert, cactus) is a place with very little water.

6. The air in a desert can be hot or (wet, cold).

7. Many desert animals look for food at (night, noon) when the air is cool.

Life Science
Core Skills Science, Grade 1

What Lives in a Desert?

Write your answers below.

8. **Vocabulary** What is a place with very little water called?

_____

9. **Reading Skill** Why do many desert plants have waxy skins?

_____

_____

_____

10. **Infer** Where do most desert animals stay during the day?

_____

_____

How Can We Help Earth?

A natural resource is something from Earth that people use.

Water, trees, and air are natural resources.

You can help save natural resources.

You can reuse, or use something again.

Reuse a milk jug.

You can make a bird feeder with it.

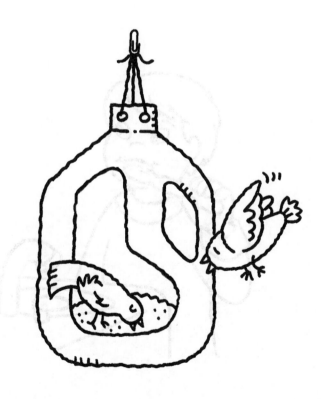

You can recycle.

A new object is made from something old when you recycle.

You can recycle old cans.

Old cans are made into new cans.

You can reduce, or use less of something.

You can turn off water while you brush your teeth.

Name _____ Date _____

How Can We Help Earth?

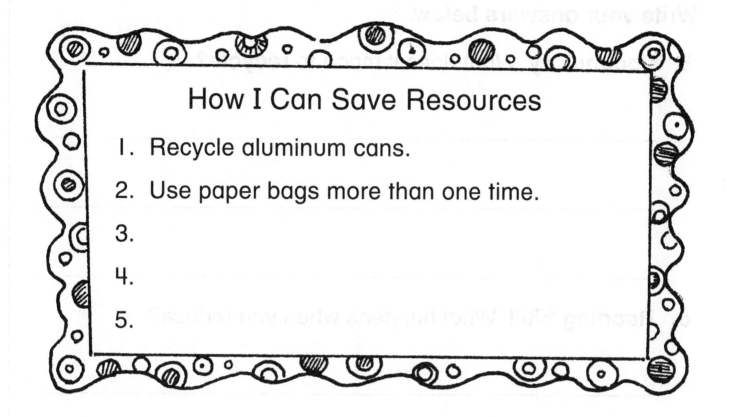

How I Can Save Resources

1. Recycle aluminum cans.

2. Use paper bags more than one time.

3.

4.

5.

Circle the number of the sentences that should go on the poster.

1. Use empty food cans to make pencil holders.

2. Keep the lights on.

3. Put newspapers in the recycling bin.

4. Buy larger packages instead of smaller ones.

How Can We Help Earth?

Write your answers below.

5. **Vocabulary** What does it mean to **recycle**?

_____

_____

6. **Reading Skill** What happens when you reduce?

_____

_____

7. **Classify** Do you reuse, recycle, or reduce when you use an old can as a trash can?

_____

How Can You Measure Weather?

Weather is what the air outside is like.

You can use tools to tell about weather.

A thermometer measures temperature.

Temperature is how warm or cool something is.

You wear warm clothes when the temperature is cold.

You wear lighter clothes when the temperature is hot.

You can use a tool to measure wind.

A windsock shows which way the wind blows.

It shows how hard the wind blows, too.

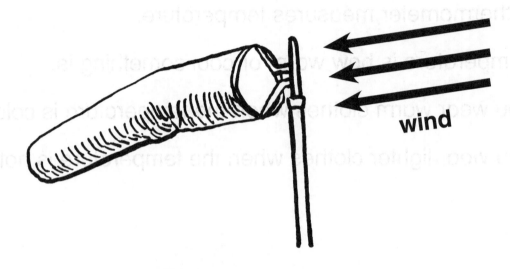

wind

windsock

You can use a tool to measure rain.

A rain gauge measures how much rain falls.

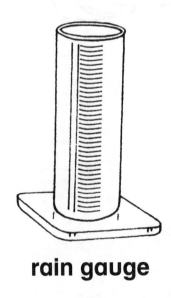

rain gauge

Earth Science
Core Skills Science, Grade 1

How Can You Measure Weather?

Draw a line from each definition to the tool it tells about.

1. a tool that measures temperature

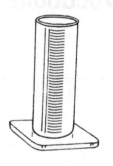

2. a tool to measure the wind

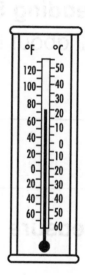

3. a tool to measure how much rain falls

How Can You Measure Weather?

Write your answers below.

4. **Vocabulary** What is **temperature**?

_____

_____

5. **Reading Skill** If a windsock is hanging down, what can you tell about the wind?

_____

_____

6. **Measure** How can you describe weather?

_____

_____

_____

Earth Science
Core Skills Science, Grade 1

What Are Clouds and Rain?

A water cycle is when water moves from Earth to the sky and back again.

The sun warms water.

Some warm water goes into the air.

You cannot see it.

Water in the air cools.

Tiny drops of water make up a cloud.

Some drops get bigger.

The drops fall to Earth as rain.

Look at clouds to see how weather changes.

Some clouds are thin.

It may rain in a day or two.

Some clouds are puffy and white.

They can turn gray and bring rain.

Some clouds are low and gray.

They may bring rain or snow.

cirrus cloud **cumulus cloud** **stratus cloud**

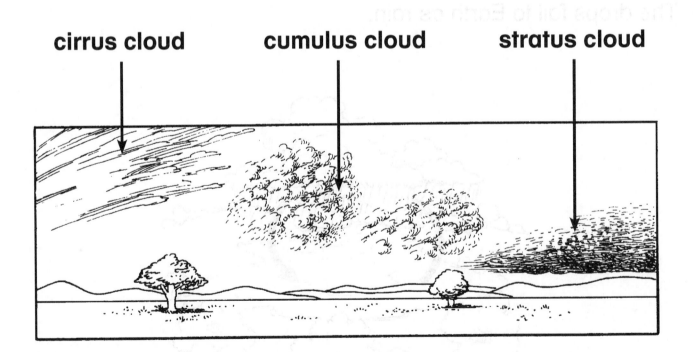

Earth Science
Core Skills Science, Grade 1

Name _____ Date _____

What Are Clouds and Rain?

Match the steps to the picture. Write the numbers 1–3 on the picture.

Steps of the Water Cycle

1. Heat from the sun causes water to go into the air.

2. Tiny drops of water in the air form clouds.

3. Water falls back to Earth as rain or sleet.

What Are Clouds and Rain?

Write your answers below.

4. **Vocabulary** What is the **water cycle**?

_____

_____

5. **Reading Skill** What causes rain to fall?

_____

_____

6. **Compare** Draw two kinds of clouds. Tell how they are alike and different.

What Is Weather Like in Spring and Summer?

A season is a time of year.

It has its own kind of weather.

Spring is the season that follows winter.

It is warmer in spring.

Warm weather and rain help plants begin to grow.

Animals that were sleeping in winter wake up.

Many baby animals are born in spring.

65

Summer is the season that follows spring.

Summer is the warmest season.

People wear clothing that keeps them cool.

Plants grow in summer.

Young animals grow bigger and learn to find food.

Soon fall comes.

The seasons change in the same order—spring, summer, fall, and winter.

What Is Weather Like in Spring and Summer?

Draw lines to match each phrase to a season.

1. season that follows winter

2. people try to keep cool

3. rain helps new plants grow

spring

4. the warmest season

5. young animals grow bigger

6. many baby animals are born

summer

What Is Weather Like in Spring and Summer?

Write your answers below.

7. **Vocabulary** What is a **season**?

_____

_____

8. **Reading Skill** How are spring and summer alike?

_____

_____

9. **Communicate** Write a story telling what happens to plants or animals in spring or summer.

_____

_____

_____

Earth Science
Core Skills Science, Grade 1

What Is Weather Like in Fall and Winter?

A season is a time of year.

It has its own kind of weather.

Fall is the season that follows summer.

It is cooler in fall.

People wear warmer clothes.

Leaves drop from trees.

Animals get ready for colder weather.

Some animals grow thick fur.

Many animals store food for winter.

Winter is the season that follows fall.

It is the coldest season.

Snow falls in some places.

Sometimes it is hard for animals to find food.

Some plants die.

Soon spring comes again.

The seasons change in the same order—spring, summer, fall, and winter.

What Is Weather Like in Fall and Winter?

Draw lines to match each phrase to a season.

1. weather gets cooler

2. some plants die

3. coldest season

4. animals grow thick fur

fall

winter

Use words from the box to name the seasons.

spring	summer	fall	winter

6. _____

5. _____

7. _____

8. _____

Name _____ Date _____

What Is Weather Like in Fall and Winter?

Write your answers below.

9. Vocabulary What is winter?

_____

_____

10. Reading Skill What season comes before fall?

_____

11. Classify Name three signs of fall.

_____

_____

What Kind of Weather Is Dangerous?

WEATHER FORECASTS

Forecast means to predict what might happen.

Some areas have bad weather.

Scientists forecast when a storm is coming.

People can take safety measures.

Sometimes power is lost during a storm.

Flashlights or candles and matches are useful.

HURRICANES

A hurricane is a huge storm that starts over the ocean.

The center of the storm is the calmest part.

A hurricane can damage buildings and trees.

If a hurricane is spotted, people should leave the area.

There are things you can do if a hurricane is coming.

Buy an emergency supply of food and water.

Cover your windows with plywood.

73

TORNADOES

A tornado is a spinning cone of air that touches the ground.

Tornadoes can be deadly.

The wind in a tornado can reach speeds of 300 miles per hour!

Stay away from windows if a tornado is spotted.

FLOODS

Floods can be caused by thunderstorms.

Too much rain may cause a river to overflow its banks.

Floodwater can enter buildings.

People should never drive into a flooded area.

People should move to higher ground.

Some areas may lose electricity until crews can repair power lines.

© Houghton Mifflin Harcourt Publishing Company

What Kind of Weather Is Dangerous?

Match each kind of weather with its description.

_____ **1.** flood

_____ **2.** hurricane

_____ **3.** tornado

a. strong winds, funnel cloud

b. high water levels

c. storm at sea that moves inland

4. Vocabulary What does it mean to forecast something?

_____

_____

_____

What Kind of Weather is Dangerous?

Write your answers below.

5. **Vocabulary** What is a tornado?

_____

_____

6. **Reading Skill** How should you prepare for a hurricane?

_____

_____

_____

7. **Infer** Why should people move to higher ground during a flood?

_____

_____

What Can You See in the Sky?

The day sky is light.

You may see clouds and birds.

You may see the sun, too.

Sometimes you may even see the moon.

The sun is the brightest object in the day sky.

It warms the land and water.

It warms the air.

You will not see other stars during the day.

The night sky is dark.

There is no light from the sun.

You can see the moon and stars at night.

Telescopes make it possible to see more stars and more detail on the moon.

Sometimes you can see planets.

A planet is an object that moves around the sun.

Earth is a planet.

What Can You See in the Sky?

Draw a line from each picture to its definition.

1. a space object that
moves around the sun

2. a space object you
can see at night and
during the day

3. the brightest space
object in the sky

Underline the word that makes the sentence true.

4. The (day, night) sky is light.

5. The (day, night) sky is dark.

Earth Science
Core Skills Science, Grade 1

What Can You See in the Sky?

Write your answers below.

6. **Vocabulary** What makes the day sky bright?

_____

_____

7. **Reading Skill** Tell one way that the sun and the moon are alike. Tell one way that they are different.

_____

_____

8. **Observe** Tell what you see in the sky.

_____

_____

What Causes Day and Night?

Earth rotates, or spins, around on an imaginary line.

This invisible line is called an axis.

The sun shines on different parts of Earth as it spins.

It is day when the part of Earth where you live faces the sun.

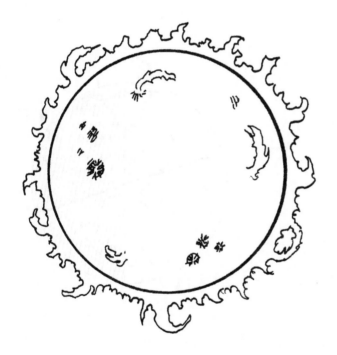

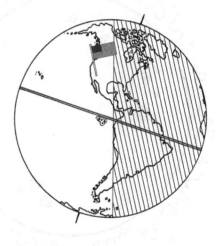

day

It is night when the part of Earth where you live faces away from the sun.

It takes 24 hours for Earth to rotate one time.

Earth keeps rotating.

Day and night repeat.

 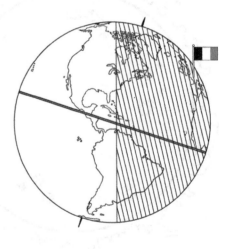

night

Name _____ Date _____

What Causes Day and Night?

1. Label the picture using words from the box.

night	day	rotates

 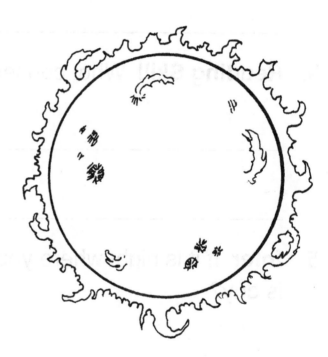

Underline the word that makes the sentence true.

2. It takes one (hour, day) for Earth to rotate one time.

Earth Science
Core Skills Science, Grade 1

What Causes Day and Night?

Write your answers below.

3. **Vocabulary** How does Earth move when it **rotates**?

_____

_____

4. **Reading Skill** What causes day on Earth?

_____

_____

5. **Infer** If it is night where you are, where do you think it is day?

_____

_____

© Houghton Mifflin Harcourt Publishing Company

Earth Science
Core Skills Science, Grade 1

How Do the Moon and Sun Seem to Change?

The moon is a round object that moves around Earth.

The moon does not make light.

The sun is a star that makes its own light.

We can see the moon because the sun shines on it.

The moon seems to change its size each night.

We see the part of the moon that the sun is shining on.

These different shapes are called the phases of the moon.

Phases of the Moon

1	2	3	4	5	6	7	8
new moon	waxing crescent	first quarter	waxing gibbous	full moon	waning gibbous	last quarter	waning crescent

The sun seems to change, too.

It seems to move from one side of the sky to the other.

The sun is not moving.

Earth is rotating and moving.

The sun is low in the sky in the morning.

It is high in the sky at noon.

It is low in the sky late in the day.

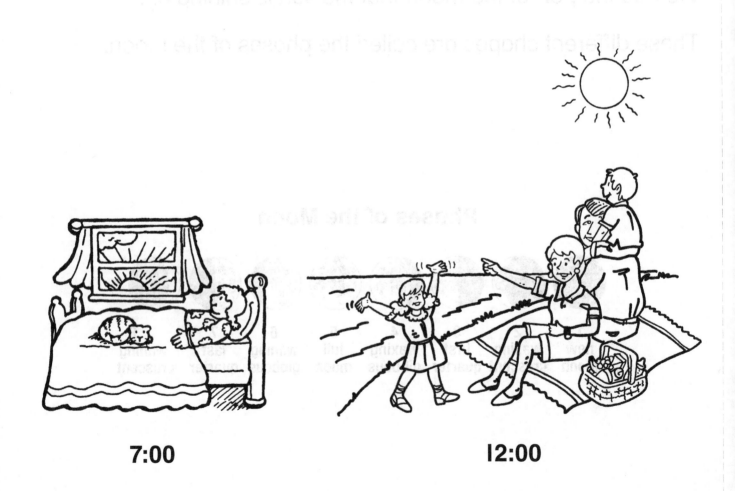

7:00   12:00

How Do the Moon and Sun Seem to Change?

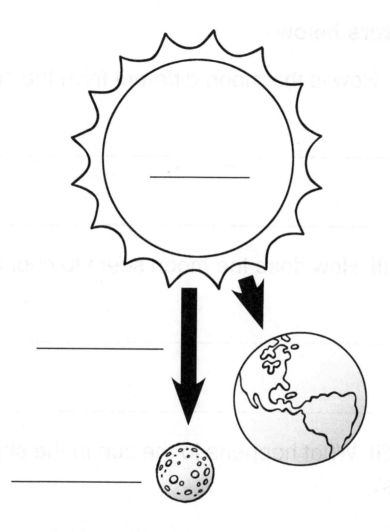

Match the sentences to the picture. Write the numbers 1–3 on the lines.

1. The sun is a star that shines on the moon.

2. Light from the sun lets us see the moon.

3. We see the part of the moon that the sun is shining on.

How Do the Moon and Sun Seem to Change?

Write your answers below.

4. **Vocabulary** How is the moon different from the sun?

_____

_____

5. **Reading Skill** How does the moon seem to change?

_____

_____

6. **Reading Skill** What happens to the sun in the sky as Earth rotates?

_____

_____

How Does Earth Move?

It looks like the sun moves, but it is Earth that moves.

Earth and other planets revolve, or move in a path, around the sun.

The path that one space object travels around another is called an orbit.

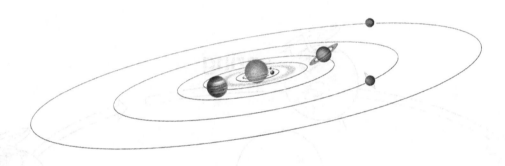

It takes one year for Earth to revolve around the sun.

Seasons are caused by the tilt of Earth's axis.

It is summer when the part of Earth tipped toward the sun gets the most light.

It is winter when the part of Earth tipped away from the sun gets less light.

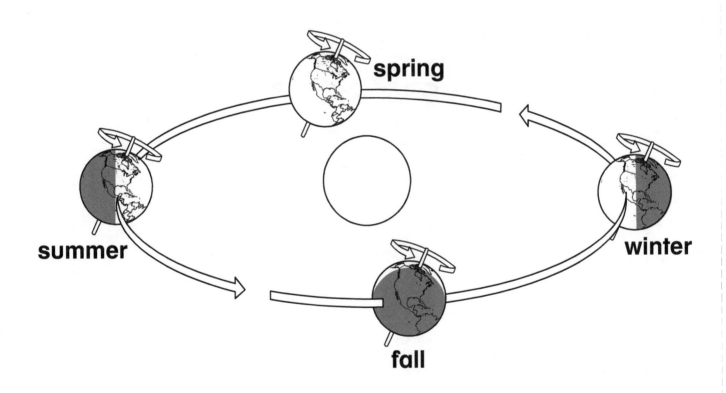

This view does not accurately show the distances between Earth and sun.

Name _____ Date _____

How Does Earth Move?

1. Label the picture using words from the box.

sun	Earth	orbit

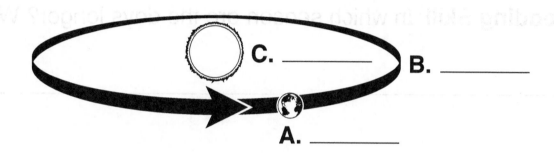

C. _____

B. _____

A. _____

Underline the word that makes the sentence true.

3. Seasons are caused by the (tilt, rotation) of Earth's axis.

Name _____ Date _____

Write your answers below.

3. **Vocabulary** Which of Earth's movements takes one year?

_____

_____

4. **Reading Skill** In which season are the days longer? Why?

_____

_____

_____

5. **Infer** If it is summer where you are, where do you think it is winter?

_____

_____

How Can You Describe Matter?

Matter is what all things are made of.

You use your senses to learn about matter.

You can see popcorn.

You can smell it.

You can touch it.

You can hear it crunch.

You can even taste it!

93

You can use your senses to tell about a property of a thing.

A property is anything you learn about an object by using your senses.

You can see the color, size, and shape of things.

You can hear how things sound.

You can tell how some things taste.

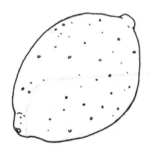

sour

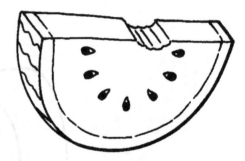

sweet

Physical Science
Core Skills Science, Grade 1

Name _____ Date _____

How Can You Describe Matter?

Draw a line from each word to its picture.

1. large

2. small

3. soft

4. rough

5. salty

6. sweet

Physical Science
Core Skills Science, Grade 1

Name _____ Date _____

How Can You Describe Matter?

Write your answers below.

7. **Vocabulary** What is **matter**?

_____

_____

8. **Reading Skill** How can your senses
help you learn about matter?

_____

_____

9. **Classify** Look at the picture.
Name two of its properties.

_____

What Are Solids, Liquids, and Gases?

Matter is what all things are made of.

There are three forms of matter.

Matter can be a solid, liquid, or gas.

A solid is matter that has its own shape.

A table and paper are kinds of solids.

You can change a solid's shape.

You can cut it.

You can break it.

solid

A liquid is matter that flows.

It takes the shape of what it is in.

Water is a liquid.

liquid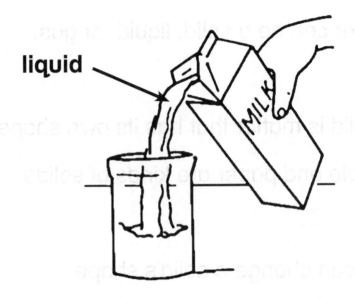

A gas is matter that changes shape to fill all the space of what it is in.

The air around you is a gas.

Gas is inside balloons, too.

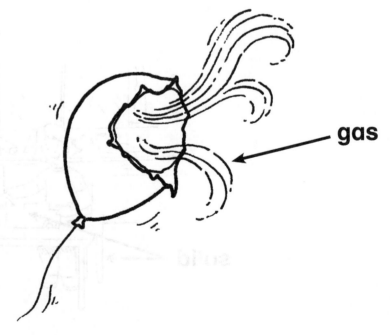
gas

What Are Solids, Liquids, and Gases?

Draw a line from each phrase to its picture.

1. has its own shape

2. fills all the space it is in

3. flows and takes the shape of its container

Underline the word that makes the sentence true.

4. Matter is what (some, all) things are made of.

5. The air around you is a (solid, gas).

Name _____ Date _____

What Are Solids, Liquids, and Gases?

Write your answers below.

6. Vocabulary What is a **solid**?

_____

_____

_____

7. Reading Skill What form of matter are milk, juice, and water?

_____

8. Compare How are solids, liquids, and gases different?

_____

_____

_____

Physical Science
Core Skills Science, Grade 1

What Do Heating and Cooling Do?

Water can change from one form of matter to another.

Water freezes when it is very cold.

To freeze is to change from a liquid to a solid.

Ice is solid water.

Solids can melt when they are heated.

To melt is to change from a solid to a liquid.

Ice melts when it gets warm.

solid

liquid

Physical Science
Core Skills Science, Grade 1

Water can be a gas, too.

Water evaporates when it is heated.

To evaporate is to change from a liquid to a gas.

You do not see water when it is a gas.

Heat from the sun makes water evaporate.

What Do Heating and Cooling Do?

1. Circle the word that tells what happened to the ice cube.

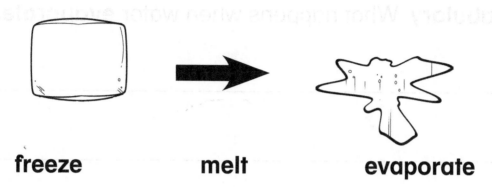

freeze   **melt**   **evaporate**

2. Circle the word that tells what happened to the water in the tray.

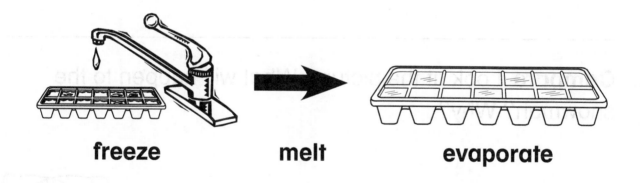

freeze   **melt**   **evaporate**

3. Circle the word that tells what happened to the water puddle.

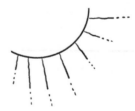

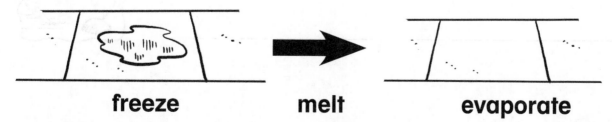

freeze   **melt**   **evaporate**

103

Physical Science
Core Skills Science, Grade 1

What Do Heating and Cooling Do?

Write your answers below.

4. **Vocabulary** What happens when water **evaporates**?

_____

_____

5. **Reading Skill** What causes liquid water to change into ice?

_____

_____

6. **Compare** Look at the picture. What will happen to the snowman? Why?

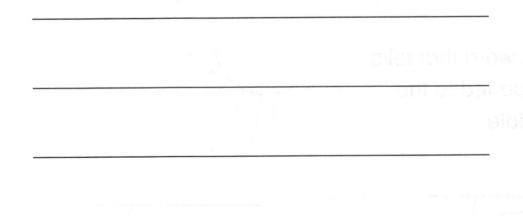

_____

_____

_____

_____

Physical Science
Core Skills Science, Grade 1

Where Does Heat Come From?

Energy is something that can cause change or do work.

Heat is a kind of energy.

Heat makes things warm.

The sun gives off heat.

The sun warms the air, water, and land.

A lightbulb gives off heat.

A fire gives off heat, too.

Heat can make things change.

Heat makes ice melt.

Heat cooks food.

Heat from a fire warms you.

Name _____ Date _____

Where Does Heat Come From?

Look at each pair of pictures. Circle the thing that has been changed by heat.

1.

2.

   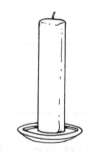

3.

Physical Science
Core Skills Science, Grade 1

Where Does Heat Come From?

Write your answers below.

4. **Vocabulary** What is energy?

   _____

   _____

5. **Reading Skill** Name three things on Earth that are heated by the sun.

   _____

   _____

6. **Compare** How is heat from the sun the same as heat from a fire?

   _____

   _____

Where Does Light Come From?

Light is a kind of energy.

Earth gets light from the sun.

Fires and lightbulbs give off light, too.

Light can pass through some things.

Light can pass through clear glass.

It can pass through air and water.

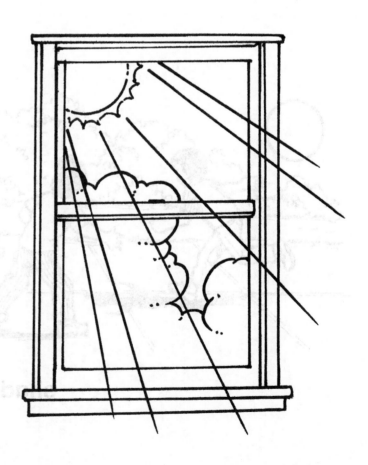

Some things let a little light through.

Sunglasses let a little light through.

Light does not pass through all things.

Some things stop all light.

Curtains can stop light.

Your body stops light, too.

A dark shape called a shadow forms when something
blocks light.

shadow

Physical Science
Core Skills Science, Grade 1

Name _____ Date _____

Where Does Light Come From?

1. Circle the things that give off light. Draw a box around the thing that does not give off light.

 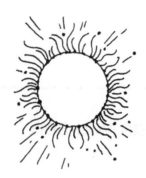 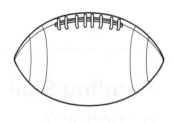

2. Write a P on the things that light can pass through. Write an S on the thing that makes a shadow.

  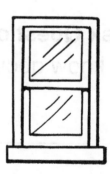

111

© Houghton Mifflin Harcourt Publishing Company

Physical Science
Core Skills Science, Grade 1

Name _____ Date _____

Where Does Light Come From?

Write your answers below.

3. **Vocabulary** What kind of energy can you see?

_____

4. **Reading Skill** Why can you see a shadow?

_____

_____

5. **Ask Questions** What else do you want to know about light and shadows?

_____

_____

Physical Science
Core Skills Science, Grade 1

How Can Light Change?

MAKING LIGHT

Some things give off light.

The sun and fire provide light as well as heat.

So do things like a flashlight and a candle.

These things need something to help them make light.

A flashlight uses batteries.

A candle burns wax.

SEEING THINGS

Objects can be seen only when there is light.

It is hard to see things in the dark.

A shadow is cast when an object blocks the light shining on it.

The light cannot reach the area of the shadow.

You can put on a puppet show by making shapes with your fingers.

Shine a light on them and cast shadows of rabbits or other animals on the wall.

Physical Science
Core Skills Science, Grade 1

LIGHT PASSING THROUGH

Some objects allow light to pass through.

Water allows some light to pass through.

Only some of the light reaches you if you are underwater.

Other objects block the light completely.

You cannot see through a solid object!

LIGHT THAT IS REDIRECTED

Mirrors and prisms redirect light.

They send light off in another direction.

A prism changes white light into a spectrum.

A spectrum is a rainbow of colors.

Some of the colors are arranged in the order Roy G. Biv.

This stands for red, orange, yellow, green, blue, indigo, violet.

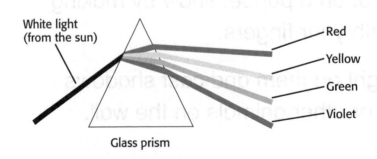

White light
(from the sun)

Red

Yellow

Green

Violet

Glass prism

Physical Science
Core Skills Science, Grade 1

How Can Light Change?

1. Draw a box around the objects that produce light.

2. Draw a circle around the objects that block light and cast a shadow.

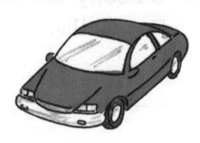

Physical Science
Core Skills Science, Grade 1

Name _____ Date _____

Write your answers below.

3. **Vocabulary** What does a prism do?

_____

_____

4. **Classify** List the colors in the spectrum in order using Roy G. Biv.

_____

_____

_____

5. **Reading Skill** How is a shadow cast?

_____

_____

6. **Contrast** How is a mirror different from a prism?

_____

_____

How Is Sound Made?

Sound is a kind of energy that you can hear.

Sound is made when something vibrates.

To vibrate means to move back and forth very fast.

You make a sound when you talk.

Place your hand on your neck.

Now sing or talk.

You can feel your neck vibrate.

How can you hear sound?

Think about a drum.

A drum vibrates when you hit it.

The air around the drum vibrates, too.

Air that vibrates makes parts inside your ear vibrate.

Then you hear sound.

Name _____ Date _____

How Is Sound Made?

1. Write an S on the objects that are making sound.

  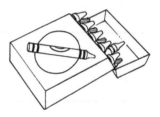

Circle the word that makes the sentence true.

2. The kind of energy you can hear is called (sound, light).

3. Sound is made when something (vibrates, shines).

How Is Sound Made?

Write your answers below.

4. **Vocabulary** What is sound?

_____

_____

5. **Reading Skill** How do you hear sound?

_____

_____

_____

6. **Observe** If you see something vibrate, what will you hear?

_____

_____

Why Are Things Fast and Slow?

Speed is how fast or slow something moves.

A train moves fast.

A snail moves slow.

Something that is moving from one place to another is in motion.

A force can change the motion of something.

You can make a ball roll faster if you kick it harder.

You stop a ball when you catch it.

Physical Science
Core Skills Science, Grade 1

A ball is light.

It is easy to stop.

It is easy to move.

Some things are heavy.

Heavy things are hard to stop.

You have to use more force to stop them.

Heavy things are hard to move, too.

You have to use more force to move them.

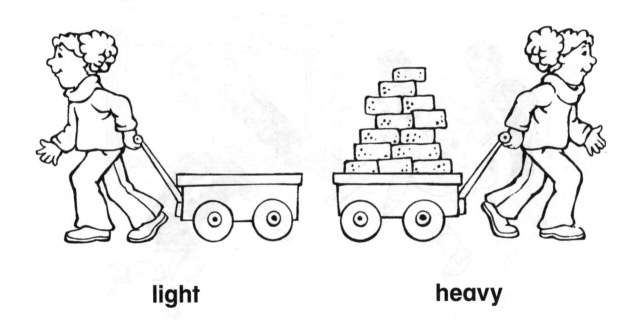

light   **heavy**

Physical Science
Core Skills Science, Grade 1

Name _____ Date _____

Why Are Things Fast and Slow?

1. Circle the thing that moves at a slow speed.

2. Circle the picture that shows something changing direction.

3. Circle the thing that you will need more force to move.

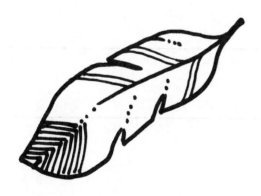   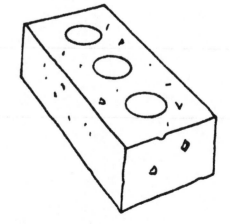

Physical Science
Core Skills Science, Grade 1

Why Are Things Fast and Slow?

Write your answers below.

4. **Vocabulary** What word tells how fast or slow
an object moves?

_____

5. **Reading Skill** What are you doing when you catch a ball?

_____

_____

_____

6. **Compare** Compare moving a heavy book
and a light book.

_____

_____

Physical Science
Core Skills Science, Grade 1

How Can We Communicate?

COMMUNICATION DEVICES

People use technology to communicate.

The telegraph was used to send short messages in the 1800s.

Telegraph operators used a special code of dots and dashes.

The telephone was developed later.

Early telephones used a circular dial.

Most phones today have number
pads instead.

CELL PHONES

Cell phones can be used for many things.

Many people enjoy texting family and friends.

Cell phones can also be used to play games.

People even use them to buy things.

COMMUNICATING WITH EMAIL

Many people communicate with email.

Email is short for "electronic mail."

The first email was sent in 1971.

Email was first used by the government.

Email is fast and easy to use.

People everywhere are using email now.

OTHER WAYS TO COMMUNICATE

People communicate with new technology.

Office workers use video conferencing to talk to each other.

The Global Positioning System (GPS) can help people find each other.

It is easy to find out people's opinions on the Internet.

How Can We Communicate?

Underline the word that makes the sentence true.

1. The (telephone, telegraph) was invented first.

2. Early telephones used a (circular dial, number pad).

3. Email stands for (emergency mail, electronic mail).

4. Video conferencing helps office workers communicate with (their pets, each other).

Circle the letter of the best answer.

5. What could help a hurt mountain climber communicate?

   A. the telegraph

   B. GPS

   C. a letter

6. Which communication method was developed last?

   A. email

   B. the telephone

   C. the telegraph

How Can We Communicate?

Write your answers below.

7. Vocabulary What does GPS stand for?

_____

_____

8. Reading Skill Compare the telegraph to email as a means of communication.

_____

_____

_____

9. Infer Why is email so popular today?

_____

_____

_____

Answer Key

Life Science

What Are the Parts of Plants? LS1.A
1. root
2. stem
3. leaf
4. flower
5. Stems
6. Leaves
7. the part of a plant that takes in water and holds the plant in the ground
8. to take in water that is in the ground and to hold the plant in the ground
9. stems, leaves, flowers, and seeds

How Can Plants Be Sorted? LS1.A
1. cactus
2. ivy
3. parts
4. people
5. seeds
6. cactus
7. Animals eat seeds, fruit, and leaves.
8. Sample answer: Some plants have spines. Some plants have flat leaves.

How Do Plants Change as They Grow? LS1.B
1. pinecone
2. seedling
3. seeds
4. the part in a pine tree that grows seeds
5. seedling
6. A picture can show what a plant looks like at different times in its life cycle.

How Do Plants Change During Their Life Cycles? LS.3A; LS.3B
Order: 2, 3, 1, 5, 4
6. Second picture: seedling
7. the changes that a living thing goes through
8. The seeds fall on the ground and make new plants.
9. A seedling does not have flowers or fruit.

How Do Animals Use Their Parts? LS1.A
1. owl
2. shark
3. owl and lion
4. shark
5. lion
6. Fins help a fish move in water.
7. Ears, eyes, legs, and paws help an animal find food.
8. A stinger hurts. It will make another animal go away.

Which Baby Animals Look Like Their Parents? LS2.A (GRADE 2); LS3.A; LS3.B
1. D
2. B
3. A
4. C
5. They reproduce.
6. A baby bird grows inside an egg. A baby mouse is born alive.
7. Sample answer: They all have fur, but the fur can be different colors.

Which Baby Animals Do Not Look Like Their Parents? LS3.A; LS3.B
1. B
2. E
3. D
4. C
5. A
6. the form of an insect that comes out of an egg
7. Baby frogs are called tadpoles. They grow back legs and lungs. They live on land as frogs. Baby butterflies are called larva. They look like a worm. They grow into a pupa. They grow wings and legs.
8. The parts for living in water disappear.

What Can People Do? LS1.D
1. hand
2. nose
3. ears
4. eyes
5. mouth
6. Answers may vary.
7. eat good food, exercise, and sleep
8. Answers may vary.

What Is a Living Thing?
1. boy holding baby
2. squirrel
3. boy drinking
4. cat and kitten
5. something that grows, changes, and makes others like itself
6. Answers may vary.
7. Water is a nonliving thing. It moves and takes up space, but it does not need air or food. It cannot make more water.

129

What Do Living Things Need?
LS1.C (GRADE K); ESS3.A (GRADE K)

1. sun and flowers
2. giraffe
3. mouse
4. dog
5. plants and other animals, and some eat both
6. food (sunlight), water, air, and space
7. water

What Lives in Forests? LS2.A
(GRADE 2)

1. rocks, water, bird nest, sky
2. Possible answers: plants, trees, shrubs, rabbit, hawk
3. pond
4. Possible answers: tree, bush, nest
5. a forest
6. No; different forests have different plants and animals.
7. Sample answer: They use nonliving things for shelter.

What Lives in Oceans and Wetlands? LS2.A (GRADE 2)

1. shark, crab, fish
2. hawk, alligator, heron (Please note that some students may mark crab or fish in wetlands as well.)
3. an ocean
4. An ocean is a large body of water. Wetlands have water and mud.
5. Both are wet places where plants and animals live.

What Lives in a Desert? LS2.A
(GRADE 2)

1. rattlesnake
2. cactus
3. jack rabbit
4. owl
5. desert
6. cold
7. night
8. a desert
9. to help them hold water
10. in their homes

Earth Science
How Can We Help Earth?
ESS3.A (GRADE K)

Circle 1, 3, and 4.

5. to make an object into something new
6. You use less of something.
7. reuse

How Can You Measure Weather? ESS2.D (GRADE K)

1. thermometer
2. windsock
3. rain gauge
4. how cool or warm something is
5. No wind is blowing.
6. You can use tools to measure temperature, wind, or rain.

What Are Clouds and Rain?

1-3. Check labels.
4. when water moves from Earth to the sky and back to Earth
5. Drops of water in clouds get bigger.
6. Answers may vary.

What Is Weather Like in Spring and Summer?

Spring: 1, 3, 6
Summer: 2, 4, 5

7. a time of year with its own kind of weather
8. The air gets warm.
9. Answers may vary.

What Is Weather Like in Fall and Winter?

Fall: 1, 4
Winter: 2, 3

5. summer
6. fall
7. winter
8. spring
9. the coldest season of the year
10. summer
11. Weather is cooler, leaves fall from trees, and animals grow thick fur.

What Kind of Weather Is Dangerous? ESS3.B

1. b
2. c
3. a
4. to predict, or tell what will happen
5. a spinning cone of air that touches the ground
6. Leave the area if possible, store food and water, and cover windows with plywood.
7. Floodwaters can enter buildings and cause harm.

What Can You See in the Sky?
ESS1.A

1. Saturn
2. moon
3. sun
4. day
5. night
6. the sun
7. Both are found in the sky. The sun gives off light, but the moon doesn't.
8. Answers may vary.

What Causes Day and Night?
ESS1.B

1. Check labels.
2. day
3. It spins.
4. the sun shining on part of Earth
5. It is day on the other side of Earth.

How Do the Moon and Sun Seem to Change? ESS1.A

1. sun
2. light ray
3. moon
4. The sun makes its own light. The moon does not.
5. It seems to change size because of the way the sun shines on it.
6. It seems to move across the sky.

How Does Earth Move? ESS1.B

1. A. Earth, B. orbit, C. sun
2. tilt
3. It takes one year for Earth to revolve around the sun.
4. Days are longer in summer because the part of Earth that is tipped toward the sun gets the most light.
5. at the other end of Earth

Physical Science
How Can You Describe Matter?

1. elephant
2. mouse (or rabbit)
3. rabbit (or mouse)
4. porcupine
5. popcorn
6. lollipop
7. what all things are made of
8. Your senses can help you find out how things taste, sound, feel, smell, and look.
9. Sample answers: light, soft, small

What Are Solids, Liquids, and Gases?

1. chair
2. balloon
3. glass
4. all
5. gas
6. matter that has its own shape
7. liquid
8. A solid has its own shape. Liquids and gases do not.

What Do Heating and Cooling Do?

1. melt
2. freeze
3. evaporate
4. It changes from a liquid to a gas.
5. Freezing turns water to ice.
6. The sun heats the snowman. The snowman will melt.

Where Does Heat Come From?
PS4.B

1. melted ice cube
2. burning candle
3. burning logs
4. something that can cause change or do work
5. air, land, and water
6. They both can warm up things.

Where Does Light Come From? PS4.B

1. circle: candle, sun
   box: football
2. P: glass, window; S: boy
3. light
4. Something blocks the light so it can't pass through.
5. Check questions.

How Can Light Change? PS4.B; ETS1.B

1. fire, candle, sun
2. building, car, dog
3. redirects a light beam, changes white light into a spectrum of colors
4. red, orange, yellow, green, blue, indigo, violet
5. An object blocks the light shining on it.
6. A mirror and a prism both redirect a light beam, but a prism changes white light into a spectrum.

© Houghton Mifflin Harcourt Publishing Company

How Is Sound Made? PS4.B

1. singer, bell ringing, bird
2. sound
3. vibrates
4. a kind of energy that you can hear
5. Air that is vibrating enters the ear and makes parts in the ear vibrate.
6. You will hear a sound.

Why Are Things Fast and Slow? PS2.A (GRADE K)

1. snail
2. ball being kicked
3. brick
4. speed
5. You are stopping the ball and changing its motion.
6. A light book is easier to move than a heavy book.

How Can We Communicate?
PS4.C; ETS1.A

1. telegraph
2. circular dial
3. electronic mail
4. each other
5. B
6. A
7. Global Positioning System
8. An operator sent a telegraph. Anyone can send emails. The telegraph used dots and dashes. Email uses letters.
9. Email is easy to use and is very fast.

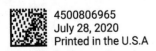